YOUR PET CAT

REVISED EDITION

A TRUE BOOK®

by
Elaine Landau

Children's Press®
A Division of Scholastic Inc.

New York Toronto London Auckland Sydney
Mexico City New Delhi Hong Kong
Danbury, Connecticut

A pile of tiny kittens

Content Consultant
Robin Downing, DVM, CVA, DAAPM
*Hospital Director, Windsor Veterinary Clinic
Windsor, Colorado*

Reading Consultant
Cecilia Minden-Cupp, PhD
*Former Director, Language and Literacy Program
Harvard Graduate School of Education*

Author's Dedication
For Pam Kelly

The photograph on the cover shows a young owner with her cat. The photograph on the title page shows a cat sitting on a tree stump.

Library of Congress Cataloging-in-Publication Data
Landau, Elaine.
   Your pet cat / by Elaine Landau — Rev. ed.
      p. cm. —   (A true book)
   Includes index.
   ISBN-10: 0-531-16766-6 (lib. bdg.)   0-531-15464-5 (pbk.)
   ISBN-13: 978-0-531-16766-3 (lib. bdg.)   978-0-531-15464-9 (pbk.)
   1. Cats—Juvenile literature. I. Title. II. Series.
SF445.7.L34 2007
636.8'083–dc22
                                                      2006004417

CHILDREN'S PRESS, and A TRUE BOOK™, and associated logos are trademarks and/or registered trademarks of Scholastic Library Publishing. SCHOLASTIC and associated logos are trademarks and/or registered trademarks of Scholastic Inc.
1 2 3 4 5 6 7 8 9 10 R 16 15 14 13 12 11 10 09 08 07

Contents

Do you think a cat makes the perfect pet? This is a British shorthair blue cat.

A Purrrrfect Pet?

Cats would rather be alone than with people. A black cat is bad luck. Cats are not friendly pets. Which of these sentences is true? In fact, none of them is true!

The truth is that cats are friendly animals that make

Cats are popular pets.

terrific pets. Did you know that people had cats as pets more than four thousand years ago? Today, cats are the most popular pets in the United States.

Why are cats such popular pets? Cats are small. They can live comfortably in a small space. Cats are not as messy as birds. They are less work than dogs. You don't have to walk your cat during a heat wave or when it gets cold.

An owner must take care of a pet's daily needs.

Cats can be cute and cuddly, but they are not toys. Getting a cat is a big responsibility. Cats need love, attention, the right food, and regular medical care. Are you ready to own a kitten or cat?

What Kind of Cat?

Are you in love with a particular **breed**, or type, of cat? Do the short-legged cats known as Munchkins make you smile? Or do you dream of owning a hairless sphynx?

Both of these are **purebred cats**. Purebred cats come

Turkish Angora (left) and Bengal (right) are two types of purebred cats.

from a long line of cats that look and act very much like one another. Purebred cats can be fun to look at, but they may not be the best choice for a pet.

Purebred cats can be expensive. Some cost thousands of dollars. They are also likely to have more health problems than **mixed-breed cats**. That's because closely related parents can pass more diseases to their young.

A Designer Cat

A sphynx cat

Breeders often mate different kinds of cats to produce new breeds. A popular breed is a hairless, or nearly hairless, cat called the sphynx.

Does a hairless cat feel chilly on a cold day? Yes, it does! A sphynx feels just as you would without your clothes. It looks for a cozy spot in the house. A hairless cat can get sunburned, too. They must be protected from too much sun. Owners love these affectionate cats that look like they came from outer space!

A mixed-breed cat is a mixture of different breeds. You can find a mixed-breed cat for a small fee at your local animal shelter. People who adopt a pet from an animal shelter often save its life.

This cat in an animal shelter waits to be adopted.

Taking Home a Healthy Cat

Before you take your new pet home, check that the cat has:

▲ a thick, glossy, smooth coat

* clean, pink ears (A cat that scratches its ears or shakes its head may have ear mites, tiny creatures that feed on other animals.)

* healthy, pink gums

* a clean, dry tail area

clear, bright eyes ▶
and a clean, moist nose

◀ a good nature and
personality (You will
want a cat that isn't
too shy or too
aggressive. Kittens
should be active
and playful.)

Your cat will need a sturdy bowl for its food.

Supplies for Your Cat

Be prepared when you bring your cat home. You will need these basic supplies:

Food and water bowls: Pick bowls that will not tip over easily. It is important to keep your cat's food and water bowls clean.

Cat brush and comb: Brush and comb a short-haired cat about once a week. Long-haired cats need brushing every day and combing once a week.

Litter box: The litter box is your cat's bathroom. Keep it in a spot your cat can easily get to. Don't put a litter box near where your cat eats or sleeps.

Kitty litter: **Kitty litter** is a material used in litter boxes to absorb moisture and reduce odors. Fill your cat's litter box with about 2 inches (5 centimeters) of litter. Remember to change the litter once a week.

A litter box with a scoop
helps keeps your house clean.

Litter scoop: Use the scoop
to remove soiled litter from
the box and put it in the
garbage. Do this twice a day.

Cat carrier: Your cat should travel in a carrier on all car trips, even short ones. It can be dangerous for a pet to walk freely in a moving car.

Cats should travel in a carrier to stay safe in the car.

Collar with an identification tag: Your cat needs to wear a collar with an identification tag attached. Some pet owners have a tiny microchip implanted under the cat's skin. If the pet is ever lost, the person who finds it can take it to an animal clinic with a scanner. Scanners can read identification information from the chip.

Scratching post: All cats need to scratch and sharpen

A kitten sharpens its claws on a scratching post.

their claws regularly. Get a sturdy scratching post with a rough surface.

A playful kitten bats a cat toy with its paw.

Cat toys: Cats play with toys
to prevent boredom. Toys also
help a cat exercise and stay

healthy. Pet stores sell lots of different cat toys. Make sure any toy you buy won't break apart. Cats can choke on small pieces.

You don't need to spend a lot of money on cat toys. Cats love to pounce on balls of crumpled paper. They also like cardboard boxes, wooden thread spools, and even big paper bags. Your cat is likely to want you to join in the fun!

Cat Care and Safety

Every cat needs a good **veterinarian**. Veterinarians are doctors who treat animals. A veterinarian checks the cat's general health and gives **vaccinations**. Vaccinations are shots that protect your cat against dangerous diseases.

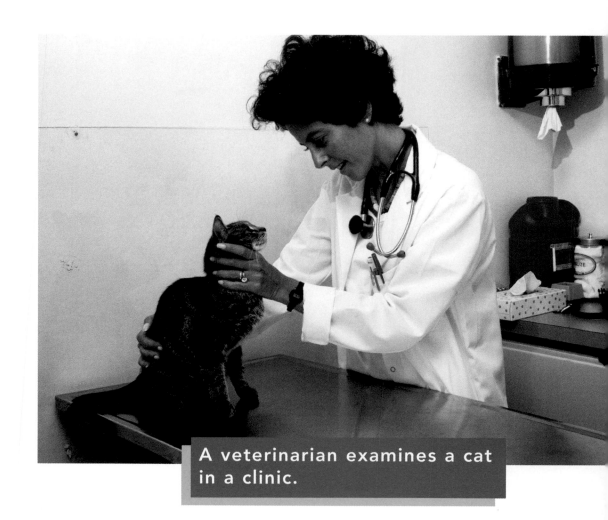

A veterinarian examines a cat in a clinic.

You should take your cat to the veterinarian for a checkup every year.

A cat cleans, or grooms, itself with its tongue.

Cats also need to be cleaned, or **groomed**. Cats are naturally clean. They wash their fur with their rough tongues about 15 percent of the day. But they also need brushing to remove dead hairs.

Brushing reduces shedding, which means fewer cat hairs on your clothes and furniture. Regular brushing also means that your cat will swallow less hair as it grooms itself. This will result in fewer **hairballs**.

An owner combs her Persian cat.

You can feed your cat dry food (top) or wet food from a can (bottom).

Hairballs are clumps of fur that form in a cat's stomach. When they become too big, the cat spits them up.

Many different kinds of cat food are available. You can choose dry cat food. That's like the dry cereal you eat for break-fast. Or you can choose canned cat food. Canned food is moist and easy to chew. When you first bring your cat home, con-tinue to feed it the same kind of food it has been eating.

Your cat's veterinarian should be able to answer your questions about pet care.

Ask your veterinarian to recommend the best food for

your pet when you go for your first visit. Never change an animal's diet suddenly unless your veterinarian recommends it.

It is better to make a gradual change. Mix the new food in with the old. Use a little more of the new food each day until you have switched to the new food entirely.

Kittens should be fed three or four times a day. Older cats usually eat twice a day.

Cats need fresh water every day.

Feed your cat at the same time in the same place every day. Cats benefit from a routine. Provide fresh food every day for your cat or kitten. Give your cat fresh water often.

Don't feed your cat or kitten table scraps or treats such as ice cream, chocolate, or cake. Most cats love people food, but some foods can be unhealthy and hard for the animal to digest. Your cat could also choke on certain foods from your table.

Responsible pet owners keep their cats safe by preventing accidents. Keep houseplants where your cat can't reach them. Eating certain houseplants can be poisonous for cats.

Keep all chemicals and household cleaning fluids in cabinets that lock or close tightly. Make sure your cat can't get to them. A taste of these products could make your cat very ill.

Your cat depends on you to keep it safe.

Cats love to sit or nap on windowsills. Make sure your windows and screens close tightly. You want your cat to remain safely inside the house.

Cats often nap in windowsills, so make sure your windows close properly.

Some people let their cats wander outdoors. Cats kept indoors are safer and usually live longer, however.

There are many dangers to letting your pet roam outside. A wandering cat can be hit by cars, attacked by dogs or other cats, or poisoned by garden chemicals. Outdoor cats are also more likely to pick up dangerous diseases from other outdoor animals.

Your New Pet

Bringing a new pet home can be exciting. If you get a kitten, you will see it grow and develop rapidly during its first year of life.

That first year of your kitten's life is about equal to fifteen years of a human's life.

Kittens grow rapidly in their first year of life.

Your cat is no longer a kitten after its first birthday. It is a teenager!

Your kitten will quickly become your best friend.

The average cat will live for twelve to fifteen years. You will be getting older, too, and you might have new interests and friends. Your cat will continue to need your time, attention, and love, however. You will still be its best friend.

Cats and kittens are wonderful creatures. Treat your new pet with kindness and respect, and it will repay you with happy memories for many years to come.

To Find Out More

Here are some additional resources to help you learn more about cats:

 **Books**

Cole, Lynn. **My Cat: How to Have a Happy, Healthy Pet**. NorthWord Press, 2001.

Engfer, LeeAnne. **My Pet Cats**. Lerner Publications, 1997.

Evans, Mark. **Kitten: A Practical Guide to Caring for Your Kitten**. Dorling Kindersley, 2001.

George, Jean Craighead. **How to Talk to Your Cat**. HarperCollins, 2000.

Jeffrey, Laura S. **Cats: How to Choose and Care for a Cat**. Enslow Publishers, 2004.

Jones, Annie. **All About Cats**. Chelsea House, 2005.

Walker, Niki, and Bobbie Kalman. **Kittens**. Crabtree Publishing, 2004.

⚡ Organizations and Online Sites

American Society for the Prevention of Cruelty to Animals (ASPCA)
424 East 92nd Street
New York, NY 10128
212–876–7700
http://www.aspca.org
This organization's site has good information on cat care, including tips on grooming, keeping your cat healthy, and making cat toys at home.

Cats International
193 Granville Road
Cedarburg, WI 53012
262–375–8852
http://www.catsinternational. org/
Cats International works to help cat owners better understand the nature and behavior of their cats. A free hotline helps owners with specific problems.

Humane Society of the United States
2100 L Street NW
Washington, DC 20037
202–452–1100
http://www.hsus.org/
This organization promotes the protection of all animals. Check out this site for information on pet care, pet adoption, and pet-related news.

NATURE, Extraordinary Cats
http://www.pbs.org/wnet/na ture/excats/resources.html
See video clips from "Extraordinary Cats," an episode in the Public Broadcasting System series *Nature*. The site also offers information about unusual cat breeds, cat photos to download, and useful links and books.

Important Words

breed a specific type of animal

groom to clean an animal

hairballs clumps of fur that form in a cat's stomach that the cat spits up

kitty litter a material used in litter boxes to absorb moisture and reduce odors

mixed-breed cats cats that are a mixture of different breeds

purebred cats cats from a long line of cats that look and act much like one another

vaccinations shots that protect animals from diseases

veterinarian a doctor who cares for animals

Index

Meet the Author

Award-winning author Elaine Landau worked as a newspaper reporter, an editor, and a youth-services librarian before becoming a full-time writer. She has written more than 250 nonfiction books for young people, including True Books on dinosaurs, animals, countries, and food. Ms. Landau has a bachelor's degree in English and journalism from New York University as well as a master's degree in library and information science. She lives with her husband and son in Miami, Florida.